Poems, Rhymes and Songs

Bridge to CURSIVE LEVEL 2

Table of Contents

Review

Lessons

Introduction

This workbook provides additional cursive practice and instruction for students who completed the first level of CursiveLogic in 2nd grade or earlier. CursiveLogic: Poems, Rhymes, and Songs provides a bridge to CursiveLogic Level 2, which is intended for use in the 4th grade. For additional materials that teach the CursiveLogic method, visit www.cursivelogic.com.

A Book of Poems to Practice and Learn

Now that you have learned to write in cursive, it is time to put your new skill to use. In this workbook, you will find many famous poems and songs that have been learned by generations of children before you. Copying and memorizing these much-loved rhymes will not only give you a chance to practice your handwriting, it will help you to become a better speaker and writer of the English language. You will learn new words and see interesting word patterns that the authors used to make their points. You might even get some ideas for writing a poem of your own! Each poem has several different kinds of exercises — tracing, reading, and writing — and may take several days to complete.

How Your Workbook Works

Your workbook is spiral-bound at the top so that it works equally well for left-and right-handed students. You will never have to rest your wrist on the coil.

Here are tips for going forward in this top-bound book. When you are viewing a BLUE page number, TURN THE PAGE. When you are viewing a MAUVE page number, FLIP THE BOOK. The arrows (↑/⟶) will remind you either to turn or flip.

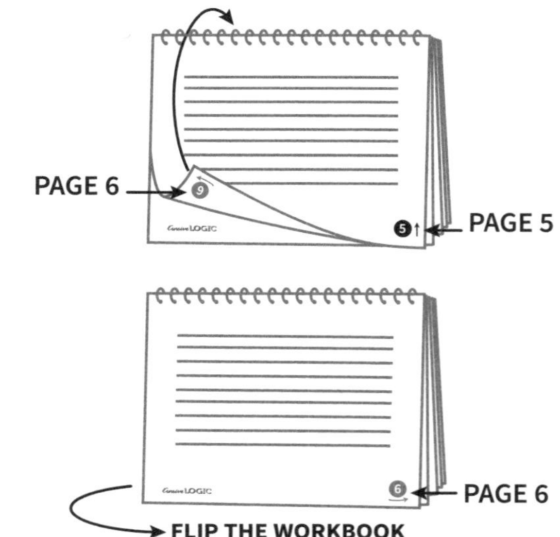

Ready, Set, Review!

It may have been several months since you finished your CursiveLogic workbook. Before you dive into the poems, take some time to review your writing technique, the four CursiveLogic letter strings, midline connections, and the uppercase letters.

Check Yourself

CHECK YOURSELF:	☐ Posture, Paper	☐ Triangle Hold	☐ Relaxed Hand, Light Pressure	☐ Touching the Guidelines Precisely	☐ Slant and Connections

Each lesson provides a chance for you to check your writing habits and decide for yourself whether you are doing your best work. If you are doing well in an area, give yourself a ✓ and keep up the good work! If you need to work harder, leave the box blank for now and re-evaluate after completing the second page of the lesson.

Posture, Paper

Sit with both feet on the floor. Lean in toward the paper, keeping your back straight.

A right-handed student turns slightly to the left and rotates the paper slightly counter-clockwise.

A left-handed student turns slightly to the right and rotates the paper slightly clockwise.

Are you using proper posture and paper orientation?

Triangle Pencil Hold

When practicing cursive handwriting, the way you hold your pencil makes a big difference. Here's how to do the "triangle" hold:

- Rest your pencil on the middle finger.
- Place your thumb and index finger so that the tip of the thumb is always slightly behind the tips of the other two.
- Keep the pencil tip clearly in view by keeping fingers one inch away from the pencil tip.

How are you holding your pencil? Is it a triangle hold?

Relaxed Hand, Light Pressure

Cursive should be written with a light touch. Fingers are relaxed and rounded (not bent at the knuckle). Apply just enough pressure to mark the page.

Is your hand relaxed? Are you pressing just the right amount (not too hard)?

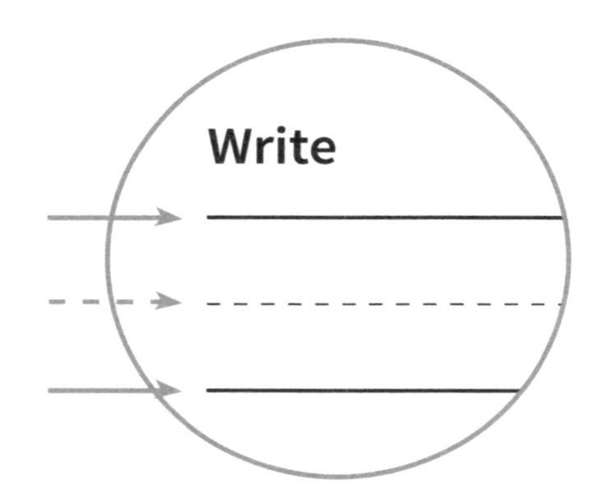

Touching the Guidelines Precisely

The guidelines used for practicing cursive have a base-, mid-, and topline that help you to make each letter exactly the right size.

Do your letters touch the guidelines precisely, without either falling short or going too far?

Slant and Connections

Look at the appearance of your writing.
Does your writing slant from left to right in the direction of movement across a page? Are the connections between your letters smooth and curved?

Think about how it feels as you write.
Does your pencil stay on the paper from the beginning of each word all the way to the end? Do you move smoothly from one letter right into the next?

Letter String Finger-Tracing

Start here (▲). Say, "OVER, BACK-TRACE [LETTER NAME] . . . DIP."

Starting on the baseline, trace the first stroke for letter 'a.' Say, **"OVER."** Pause, then back-trace and complete 'a' saying, **"BACK-TRACE [a]."**

Each time your finger touches the baseline at the end of a letter, repeat the process for the next letter without lifting your finger. For the final stroke of 'o' make a small curve under the midline and say, **"DIP."** Repeat the letter string 3 times.

Start here (▲). Say, "LOOP LEFT, DOWNSTROKE [LETTER NAME] . . . DIP."

Starting on the baseline, trace the first stroke for letter 'f' saying, **"LOOP LEFT,"** then downstroke and complete 'f' saying, **"DOWNSTROKE [f]."**

Each time your finger touches the baseline at the end of a letter, repeat the process for the next letter without lifting your finger. For the final stroke of 'b' make a small curve on the midline and say, **"DIP."** Repeat the letter string 3 times.

Start here (▲) on the baseline. Say, "SWING RIGHT [LETTER NAME] . . . DIP."

Starting on the baseline, trace the first stroke for letter 'i.' Say, "**SWING RIGHT.**" Then downstroke and complete 'i' saying, "**[i].**"

Each time your finger touches the baseline at the end of a letter, repeat the process for the next letter without lifting your finger. For the final stroke of 'w' make a small curve on the midline and say, "**DIP.**"

Dot 'i,' dot 'j' and cross 't'. Repeat for remaining three lines.

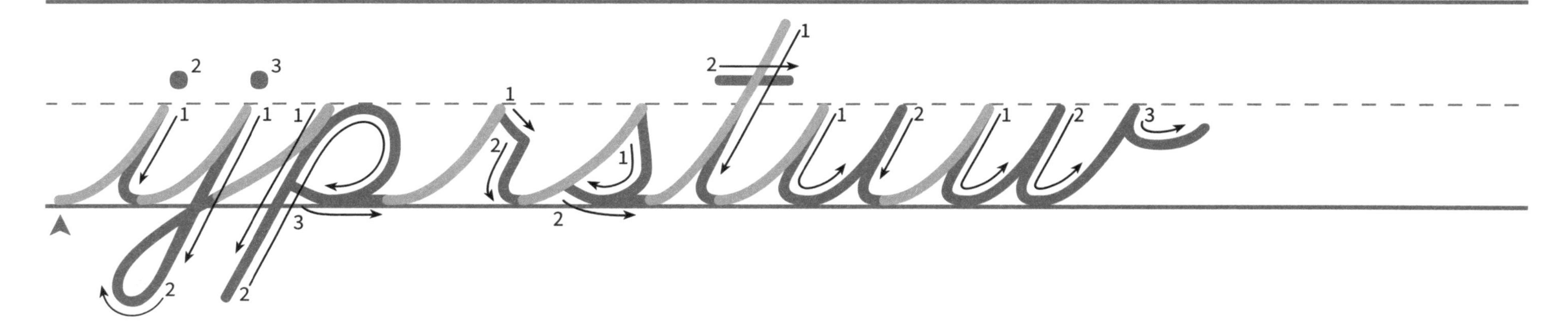

Start here (▲) on the baseline. Say, "MOUND ROUND [LETTER NAME] . . . DIP."

Beginning at the baseline, trace the first stroke for letter 'm.' Say, "**MOUND ROUND.**" Then downstroke and complete 'm' saying, "**[m].**"

Each time your finger touches the baseline at the end of a letter, repeat the process for the next letter without lifting your finger*. For the final stroke of 'v' make a small curve on the midline and say, "**DIP.**" Repeat the letter string 3 times.

* EXCEPTION: You may lift the pencil and cross 'x' while saying 'x.'

Mind Your gs and qs

Mixing up lowercase 'g' and 'q' is common because they are similar. Take a closer look at how 'g' and 'q' are alike and what strokes make them different.

LEFT

Different:

- Loop LEFT
- Upstroke RIGHT
- Cross the downstroke on the baseline to close the loop

Alike:

- Over, back-trace
- Upstroke to close
- Downstroke below the baseline

RIGHT

Different:

- Loop RIGHT
- Upstroke LEFT
- Close the loop on the baseline
- Short stroke right

After closing the oval, keep your downstroke nice and straight until it is time to loop left or right at the bottom of the letter.

TRACE

ggg qqq ggg qqq ggg qqq

WRITE

Review the Letter Strings and Catch Phrases

Each day, you will have an opportunity to review the letters strings and catch phrases before you begin your practice. Tracing through the letter strings while chanting the catch phrases will quickly remind you how to form each letter and will prepare you to complete the rest of your practice efficiently.

Take a moment to trace and write the four letter strings now. Don't forget to say the catch phrases as you trace.

TRACE

WRITE

Now practice the lowercase letters in alphabetical order. Don't chant the catch phrases this time, since the letters are not in shape order. But you can always refer back to the phrases in your mind if you need help remembering how to form a certain letter.

TRACE

WRITE

Review Midline Connections

As you practice connecting letters at the midline, say the word DIP to help remind yourself how to link the letters correctly.

o

TRACE

oa oo ob oe oi or os om

WRITE

b

TRACE

ba bo bb be bi br bs by

WRITE

w

TRACE

wa wo wh we wi wr ws wn

WRITE

v

TRACE

va vo vf ve vt vr vs vy

WRITE

Practice Midline Connections

TRACE

oats goose does old oil dot ore on

WRITE

TRACE

bar bow able bit bray sobs flabby

WRITE

TRACE

warm wolf wet whale wrap stows

WRITE

TRACE

vault voice love view gravy

WRITE

CHECK YOURSELF: ☐ Posture, Paper ☐ Triangle Hold ☐ Relaxed Hand, Light Pressure ☐ Touching the Guidelines Precisely ☐ Slant and Connections

Capital Letter Finger-Tracing

Start here (•). Say, "Capital [LETTER NAME]."

Start Point: Under the topline

First Stroke: Curve left

A C E O Q

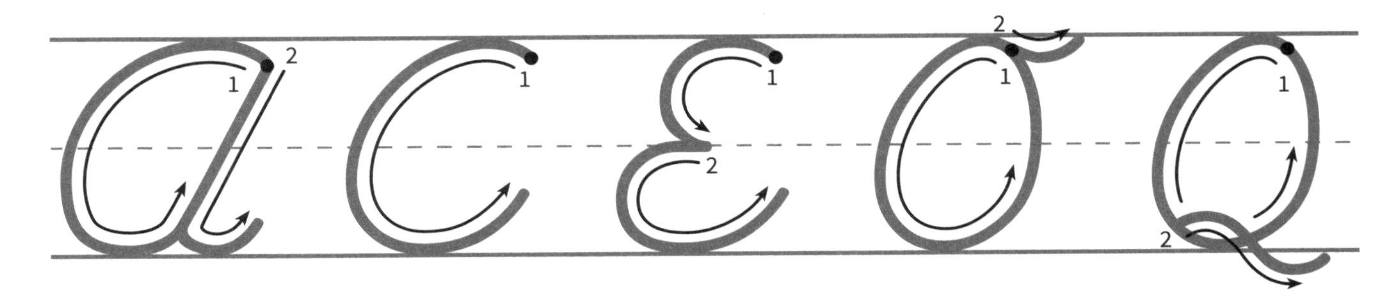

Start Point: Baseline

First Stroke: G and S — slant right, loop left;
I and J — loop right

G S I J

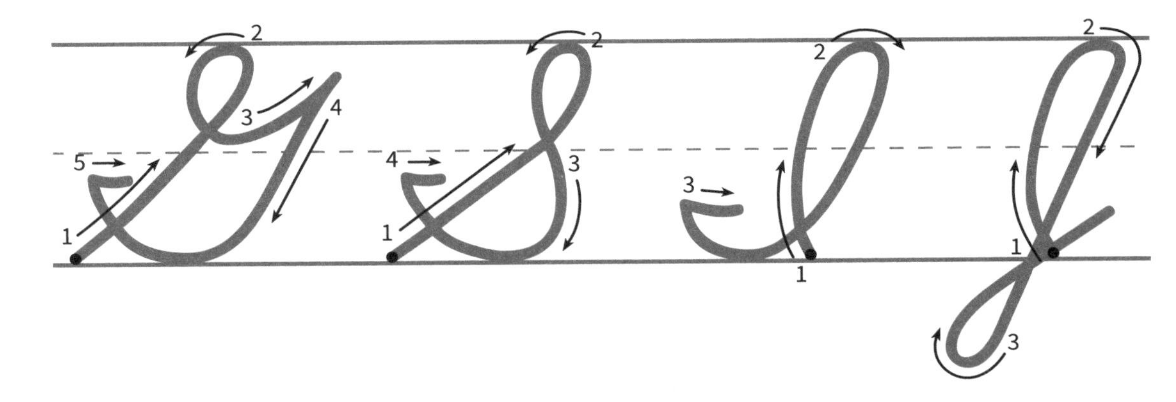

Start Point: Under the topline

First Stroke: Over curve & straight stroke to baseline

B P R M N

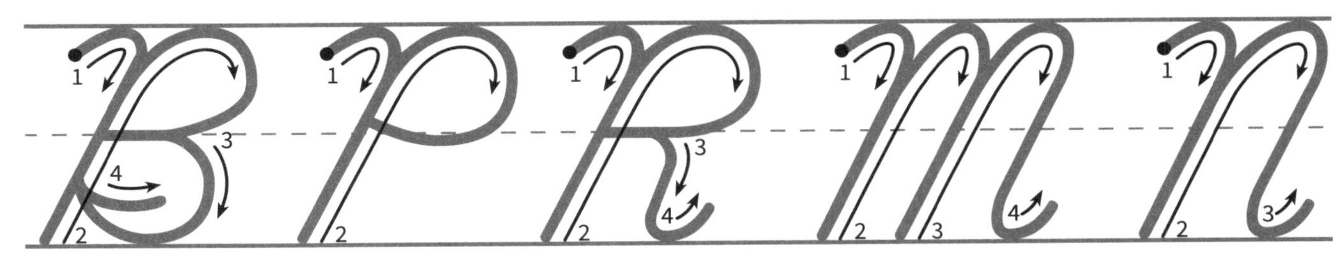

Practice Capital Letters

TRACE

A C E O Q

WRITE

TRACE

G S I J

WRITE

TRACE

B P R M N

WRITE

TRACE

A C E O Q

WRITE

TRACE

G S I J

WRITE

TRACE

B P R M N

WRITE

Capital Letter Finger-Tracing

Start here (•). Say, "Capital [LETTER NAME]."

Start Point: Under the topline

First Stroke: Over curve to baseline curve

U V W Y

Start Point: Under the topline

First Stroke: Plus 1 or more pencil lifts

H K X T F

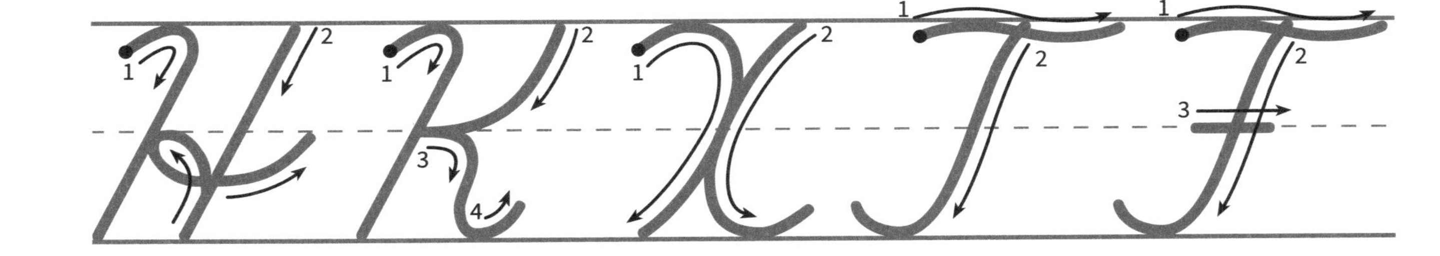

Start Point: Under the topline

First Stroke: Miscellaneous

D L Z

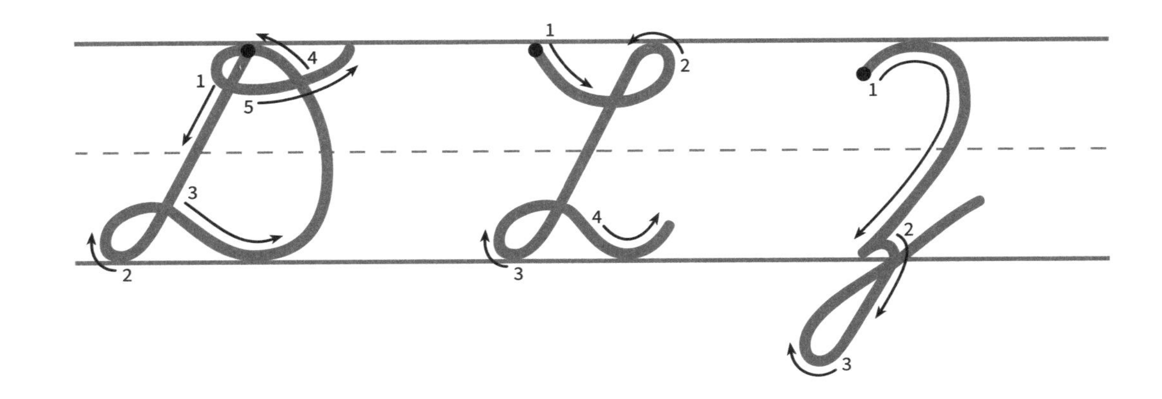

Practice Capital Letters

TRACE

U V W Y

WRITE

TRACE

H K X T F

WRITE

TRACE

D L Z

WRITE

TRACE

U V W Y

WRITE

TRACE

H K X T F

WRITE

TRACE

D L Z

WRITE

OVER, BACK-TRACE   LOOP LEFT, DOWNSTROKE   SWING RIGHT   MOUND ROUND

acdgqofhklebijprstuwvmnxyzv

TRACE

Bed in Summer Robert Louis Stevenson

In winter I get up at night
And dress by yellow candle-light.
In summer, quite the other way,
I have to go to bed by day.

I have to go to bed and see
The birds still hopping on the tree,
Or hear the grown-up people's feet
Still going past me in the street.

And does it not seem hard to you,
When all the sky is clear and blue,
And I should like so much to play,
To have to go to bed by day?

WRITE

Focus on Ovals

Trace the letter string with your finger three times. Go slowly and be sure you are tracing each letter perfectly.

Start here (▲). Say, **"OVER, BACK-TRACE [LETTER NAME] . . . DIP."**

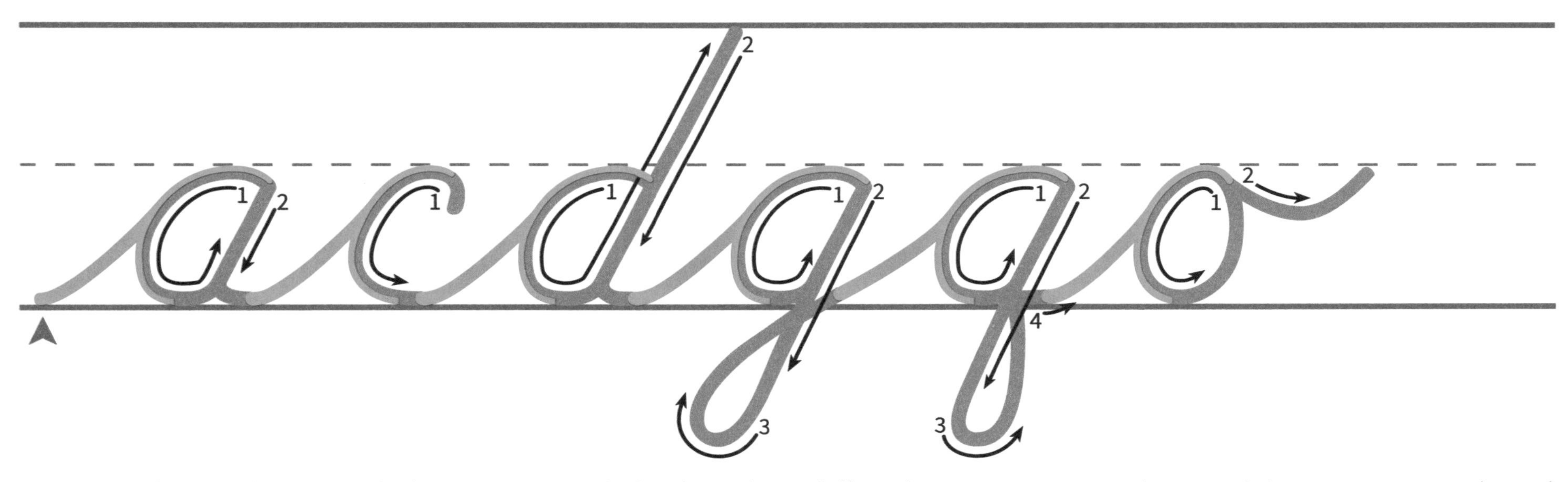

Now complete each exercise below. Again, work slowly and carefully to be sure you are making each letter as accurately and beautifully as you can. You can speed back up on the next poem.

Start here (▲). Say, **"OVER, BACK-TRACE [LETTER NAME] . . . DIP."**

TRACE

acdgqo acdgqo acdgqo acdgqo

WRITE

Start here (▲). Say, "OVER, BACK-TRACE [LETTER NAME] . . . DIP."

TRACE

acdggo acdggo acdggo acdggo

WRITE

TRACE

acdggo acdggo acdggo acdggo

WRITE

WRITE

WRITE

CHECK YOURSELF: ☐ Posture, Paper ☐ Triangle Hold ☐ Relaxed Hand, Light Pressure ☐ Touching the Guidelines Precisely ☐ Slant and Connections

OVER, BACK-TRACE LOOP LEFT, DOWNSTROKE SWING RIGHT MOUND ROUND

acdgqofhklebijprstuwmnxyzv

TRACE

Mr. Nobody

I know a funny little man,

As quiet as a mouse,

Who does the mischief that is done

In everybody's house!

There's no one ever sees his face,
And yet we all agree
That every plate we break was cracked
By Mr. Nobody.

CHECK YOURSELF: ☐ Posture, Paper ☐ Triangle Hold ☐ Relaxed Hand, Light Pressure ☐ Touching the Guidelines Precisely ☐ Slant and Connections

Mr. Nobody

I know a funny little man,
As quiet as a mouse,
Who does the mischief that is done
In everybody's house!

WRITE

Focus on Loops

Trace the letter string with your finger three times. Go slowly and be sure you are tracing each letter perfectly.

Start here (▲). Say, "LOOP LEFT, DOWNSTROKE [LETTER NAME] . . . DIP."

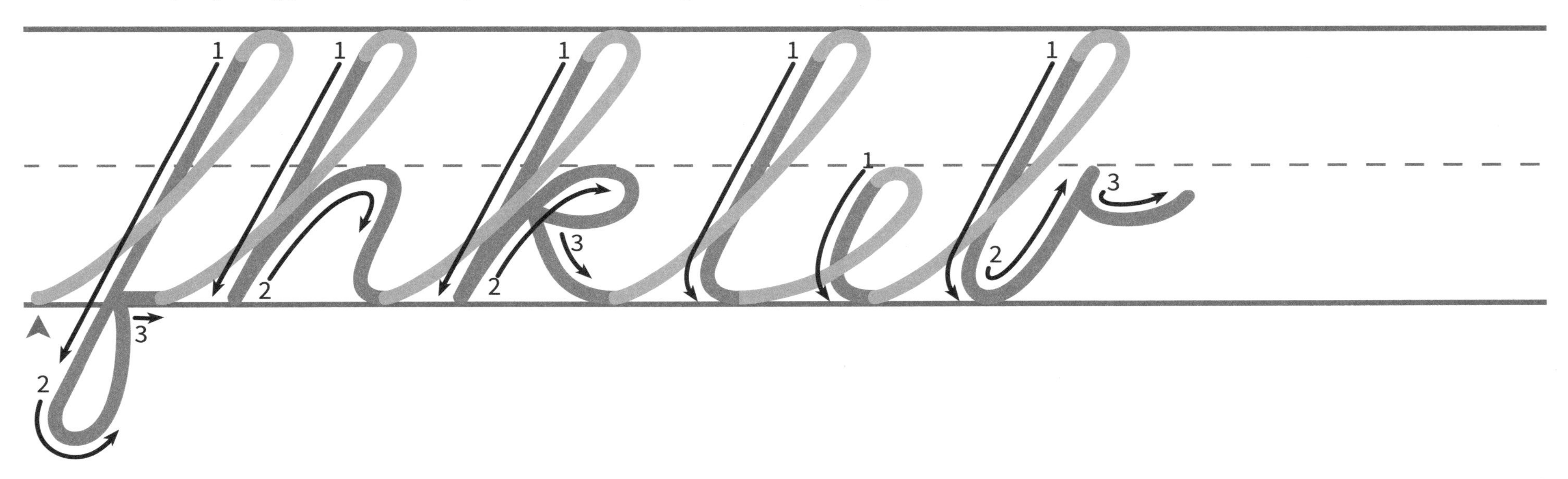

Now complete each exercise below. Again, work slowly and carefully to be sure you are making each letter as accurately and beautifully as you can. You can speed back up on the next poem.

Start here (▲). Say, "LOOP LEFT, DOWNSTROKE [LETTER NAME] . . . DIP."

TRACE

fhkleb fhkleb fhkleb fhkleb

WRITE

Start here (▲). Say, "LOOP LEFT, DOWNSTROKE [LETTER NAME] . . . DIP."

TRACE

fhkleb fhkleb fhkleb fhkleb

WRITE

TRACE

fhkleb fhkleb fhkleb fhkleb

WRITE

WRITE

WRITE

CHECK YOURSELF: ☐ Posture, Paper ☐ Triangle Hold ☐ Relaxed Hand, Light Pressure ☐ Touching the Guidelines Precisely ☐ Slant and Connections

OVER, BACK-TRACE LOOP LEFT, DOWNSTROKE SWING RIGHT MOUND ROUND

acdgqofhkleb ijpr stu w mnx yz v

TRACE

An Autumn Greeting by George Cooper

"Come, little leaves," said the wind one day—

"Come o'er the meadows with me and play;

Put on your dresses of red and gold—

Summer is gone and the days grow cold."

CHECK YOURSELF: ☐ Posture, Paper ☐ Triangle Hold ☐ Relaxed Hand, Light Pressure ☐ Touching the Guidelines Precisely ☐ Slant and Connections

An Autumn Greeting by George Cooper

"Come, little leaves," said the wind one day—
"Come o'er the meadows with me and play;
Put on your dresses of red and gold—
Summer is gone and the days grow cold."

WRITE

Focus on Swings

Trace the letter string with your finger three times. Go slowly and be sure you are tracing each letter perfectly.

Start here (▲) on the baseline. Say, "SWING RIGHT [LETTER NAME] . . . DIP."

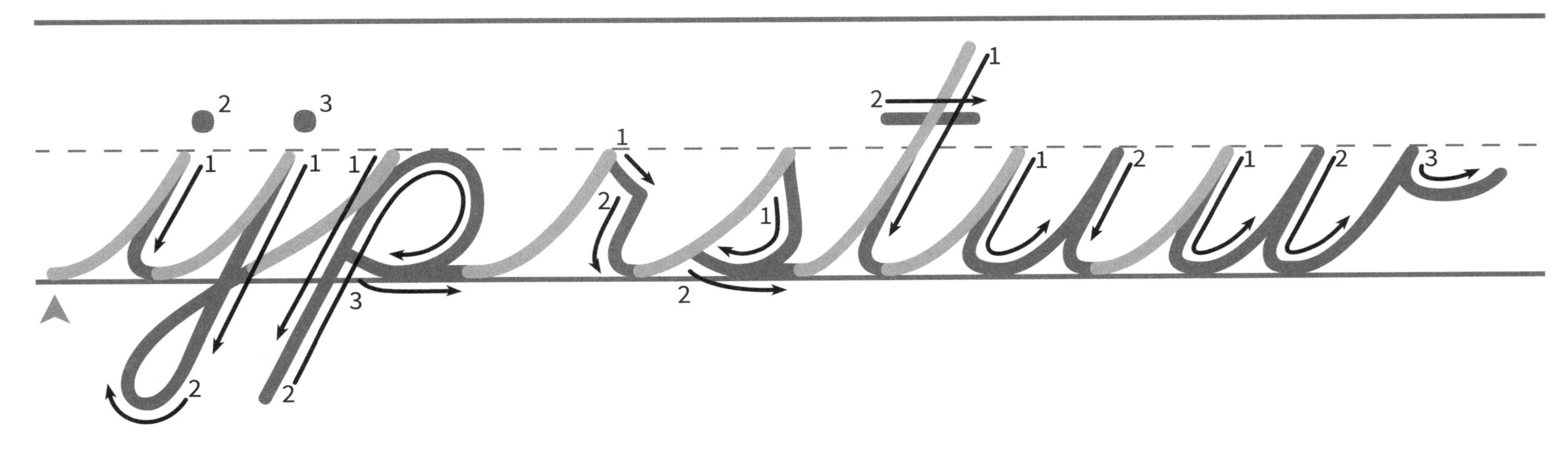

Now complete each exercise below. Again, work slowly and carefully to be sure you are making each letter as accurately and beautifully as you can. You can speed back up on the next poem.

Start here (▲). Say, "SWING RIGHT [LETTER NAME] . . . DIP."

TRACE

WRITE

Start here (▲). Say, "SWING RIGHT [LETTER NAME] . . . DIP."

TRACE

▲

WRITE

▲

TRACE

▲

WRITE

▲

WRITE

▲

WRITE

▲

CHECK YOURSELF:

Posture, Paper

Triangle Hold

Relaxed Hand, Light Pressure

Touching the Guidelines Precisely

Slant and Connections

acdgqofhkleb ijprstuwvmnxyzv

TRACE

We never know how high we are

by Emily Dickinson

We never know how high we are

Till we are called to rise;

And then, if we are true to plan,

Our statures touch the skies—

The Heroism we recite
Would be a daily thing,
Did not ourselves the Cubits warp
For fear to be a King—

We never know how high we are
by Emily Dickinson
We never know how high we are
Till we are called to rise;
And then, if we are true to plan,
Our statures touch the skies—

WRITE

Focus on Mounds

Trace the letter string with your finger three times. Go slowly and be sure you are tracing each letter perfectly.

Start here (▲) on the baseline. Say, **"MOUND ROUND [LETTER NAME] . . . DIP."**

Now complete each exercise below. Again, work slowly and carefully to be sure you are making each letter as accurately and beautifully as you can. You can speed back up on the next poem.

Start here (▲). Say, **"MOUND ROUND [LETTER NAME] . . . DIP."**

TRACE

WRITE

Start here (▲). Say, “MOUND ROUND [LETTER NAME] . . . DIP.”

TRACE

mnxyzv mnxyzv mnxyzv mnxyzv

WRITE

TRACE

mnxyzv mnxyzv mnxyzv mnxyzv

WRITE

WRITE

WRITE

OVER, BACK-TRACE   LOOP LEFT, DOWNSTROKE   SWING RIGHT   MOUND ROUND

acdgqofhkleb ijprstuwvmnxyzv

TRACE

Mary's Lamb by Sarah Josepha Hale

Mary had a little lamb,

Its fleece was white as snow;

And every where that Mary went

The lamb was sure to go;

He followed her to school one day—
That was against the rule;
It made the children laugh and play,
To see a lamb at school.

CHECK YOURSELF: ☐ Posture, Paper ☐ Triangle Hold ☐ Relaxed Hand, Light Pressure ☐ Touching the Guidelines Precisely ☐ Slant and Connections

TRACE

And so the Teacher turned him out,
But still he lingered near,
And waited patiently about,
Till Mary did appear;

WRITE

TRACE

And then he ran to her, and laid
His head upon her arm,
As if he said, "I'm not afraid—
You'll keep me from all harm."

WRITE

"What makes the lamb love Mary so?"
The little children cry—
"O, Mary loves the lamb, you know,"
The Teacher did reply;

WRITE

"And you each gentle animal
In confidence may bind,
And make them follow at your call,
If you are always kind."

OVER, BACK-TRACE LOOP LEFT, DOWNSTROKE SWING RIGHT MOUND ROUND

acdggofhklebijprstuwmnxyzv

TRACE

Nonsense by Edward Lear

There was an Old Man with a beard,
Who said, "It is just as I feared!—
Two Owls and a Hen,
Four Larks and a Wren,
Have all built their nests in my beard!"

Nonsense by Edward Lear

There was an Old Man with a beard,
Who said, "It is just as I feared!-
Two Owls and a Hen,
Four Larks and a Wren,
Have all built their nests in my beard!"

WRITE

Practice Midline Connections

TRACE

poster coat frog about bother door

WRITE

TRACE

tubs debt bye baby able bowl

WRITE

TRACE

week who owl hawk away yawn

WRITE

TRACE

voice voyage view vein

WRITE

Practice Midline Connections

TRACE

over ozone oxen omen order

WRITE

TRACE

bubble brag boss bite boil

WRITE

TRACE

wrist paws wars worth wool crowd

WRITE

TRACE

valve vroom envy savvy

WRITE

OVER, BACK-TRACE LOOP LEFT, DOWNSTROKE **SWING RIGHT** MOUND ROUND

acdggofhklebijjprstuwmnxyzv

TRACE

Over the River and Through the Wood

by Lydia Maria Child

Over the river, and through the wood,

To Grandfather's house we go;

the horse knows the way to carry the sleigh

through the white and drifted snow.

Over the river, and through the wood—
oh, how the wind does blow!
It stings the toes and bites the nose
as over the ground we go.

CHECK YOURSELF: ☐ Posture, Paper ☐ Triangle Hold ☐ Relaxed Hand, Light Pressure ☐ Touching the Guidelines Precisely ☐ Slant and Connections

Over the river, and through the wood –
and straight through the barnyard gate,
We seem to go extremely slow,
it is so hard to wait!

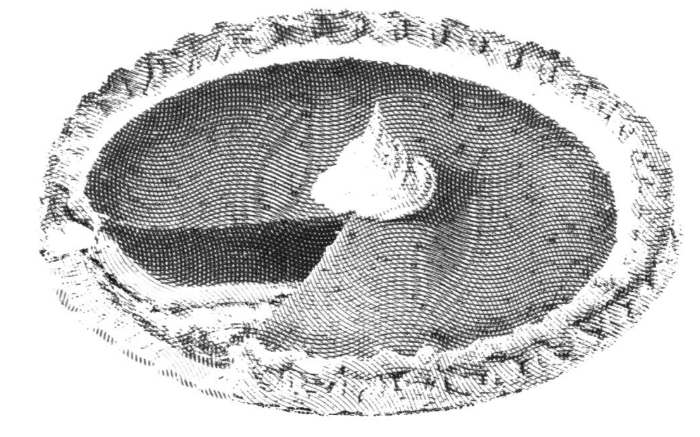

WRITE

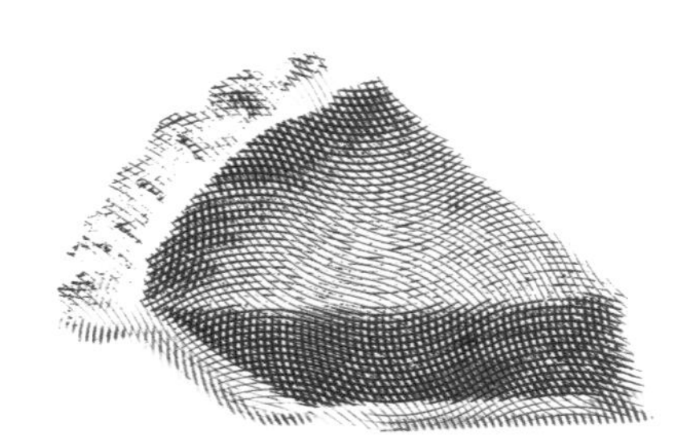

Over the river, and through the wood –
now Grandmother's cap I spy!
Hurrah for the fun! Is the pudding done?
Hurrah for the pumpkin pie!

Practice Capital Letters

A C E O Q

Start here (●). Say, "CAPITAL [LETTER NAME]."

Finger-trace the letter group three times.

Start Point: Under the topline

First Stroke: Curve left

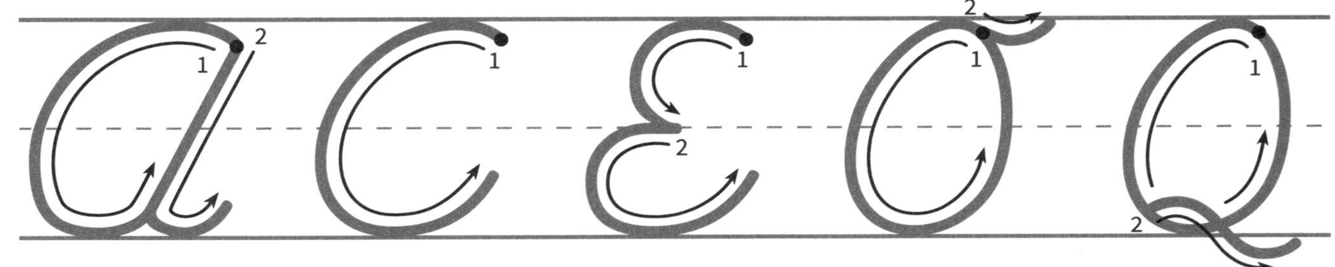

TRACE

WRITE

TRACE **WRITE**

TRACE **WRITE**

Start here (•). Say, "CAPITAL [LETTER NAME]."

Finger-trace the letter group three times.

Start Point: Under the topline

First Stroke: Curve left

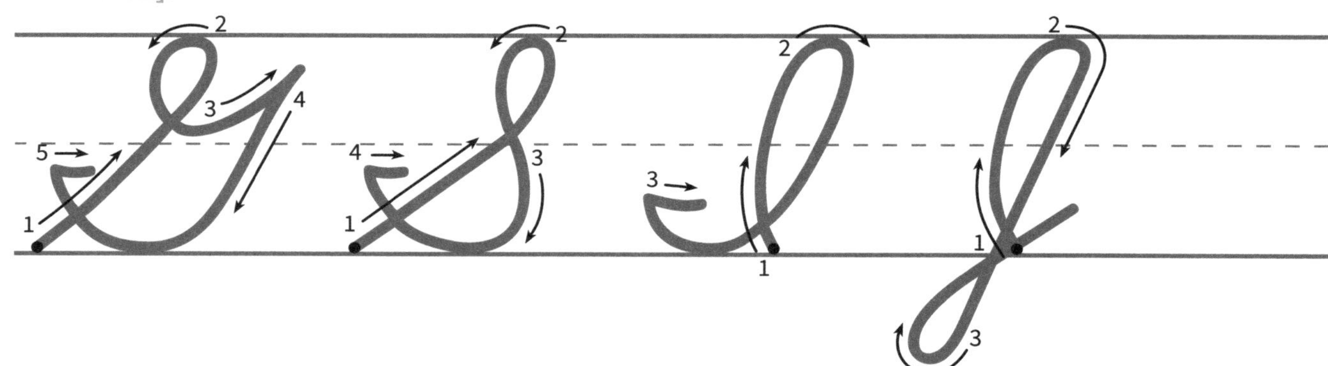

TRACE

WRITE

TRACE **WRITE**

TRACE **WRITE**

OVER, BACK-TRACE LOOP LEFT, DOWNSTROKE SWING RIGHT MOUND ROUND

acdggofhklebijjprstuwmnxyzv

TRACE

Jingle Bells by John Pierpont

Dashing thro' the snow,

In a one horse open sleigh,

O'er the hills we go,

Laughing all the way;

Bells on bob tail ring,
Making spirits bright,
Oh what sport to ride and sing
A sleighing song tonight.

CHECK YOURSELF: ☐ Posture, Paper ☐ Triangle Hold ☐ Relaxed Hand, Light Pressure ☐ Touching the Guidelines Precisely ☐ Slant and Connections

Jingle bells, Jingle bells,
Jingle all the way;
Oh! what joy it is to ride
In a one horse open sleigh.

WRITE

Practice Capital Letters

Start here (•). Say, “CAPITAL [LETTER NAME].”

Finger-trace the letter group three times.

Start Point: Under the topline

First Stroke: Curve left

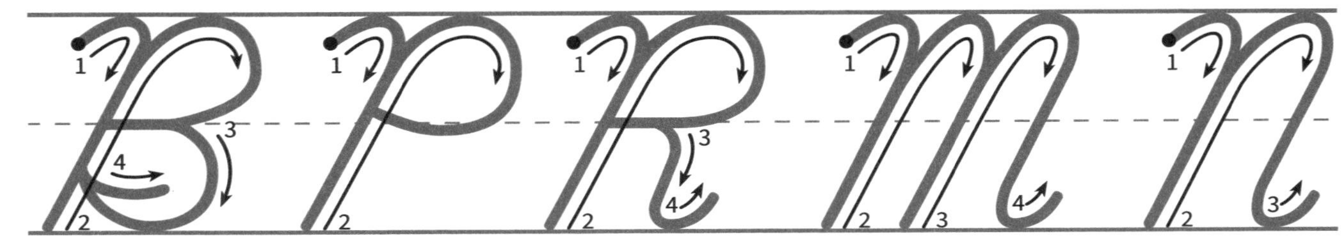

TRACE

B P R M N B P R M N B P R M N

WRITE

TRACE **WRITE**

B B B

P P P

R R R

M M M

N N N

TRACE **WRITE**

B B B

P P P

R R R

M M M

N N N

CHECK YOURSELF: ☐ Posture, Paper ☐ Triangle Hold ☐ Relaxed Hand, Light Pressure ☐ Touching the Guidelines Precisely ☐ Slant and Connections

Start here (•). Say, "CAPITAL [LETTER NAME]."

Finger-trace the letter group three times.

Start Point: Under the topline

First Stroke: Curve left

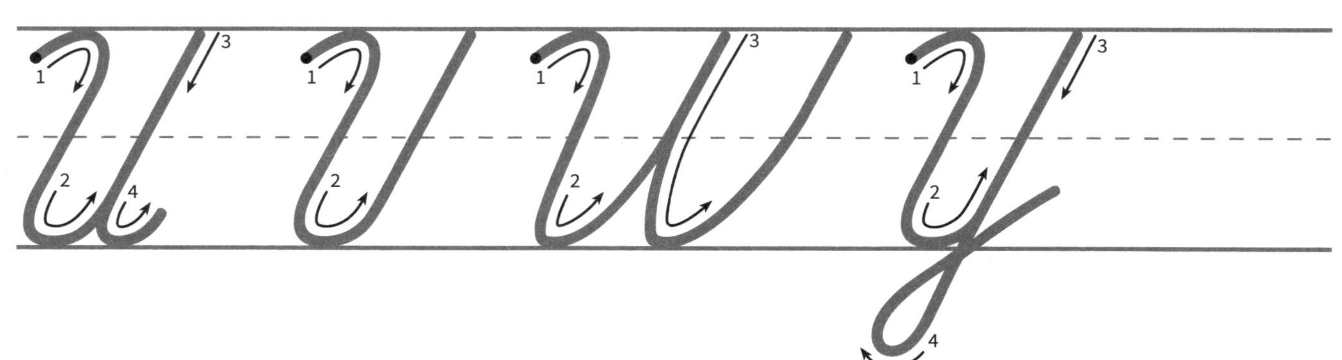

TRACE

WRITE

TRACE **WRITE**

TRACE **WRITE**

CHECK YOURSELF: ☐ Posture, Paper ☐ Triangle Hold ☐ Relaxed Hand, Light Pressure ☐ Touching the Guidelines Precisely ☐ Slant and Connections

OVER, BACK-TRACE LOOP LEFT, DOWNSTROKE SWING RIGHT MOUND ROUND

acdgqofhklebijprstuwvmnxyzv

TRACE

America the Beautiful

Katherine Lee Bates

O beautiful for spacious skies,

For amber waves of grain,

For purple mountain majesties

Above the fruited plain!

America! America!
God shed His grace on thee
And crown thy good with brotherhood
From sea to shining sea!

CHECK YOURSELF: ☐ Posture, Paper ☐ Triangle Hold ☐ Relaxed Hand, Light Pressure ☐ Touching the Guidelines Precisely ☐ Slant and Connections

America the Beautiful
Katherine Lee Bates
O beautiful for spacious skies,
For amber waves of grain,
For purple mountain majesties
Above the fruited plain!

WRITE

Practice Capital Letters

Start here (•). Say, "CAPITAL [LETTER NAME]."

Finger-trace the letter group three times.

Start Point: Under the topline

First Stroke: Curve left

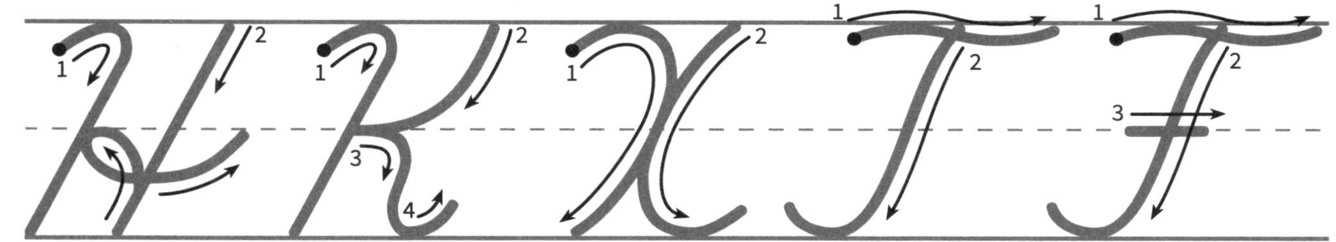

TRACE

WRITE

TRACE **WRITE**

TRACE **WRITE**

Start here (•). Say, "CAPITAL [LETTER NAME]."

Finger-trace the letter group three times.

Start Point: Under the topline

First Stroke: Curve left

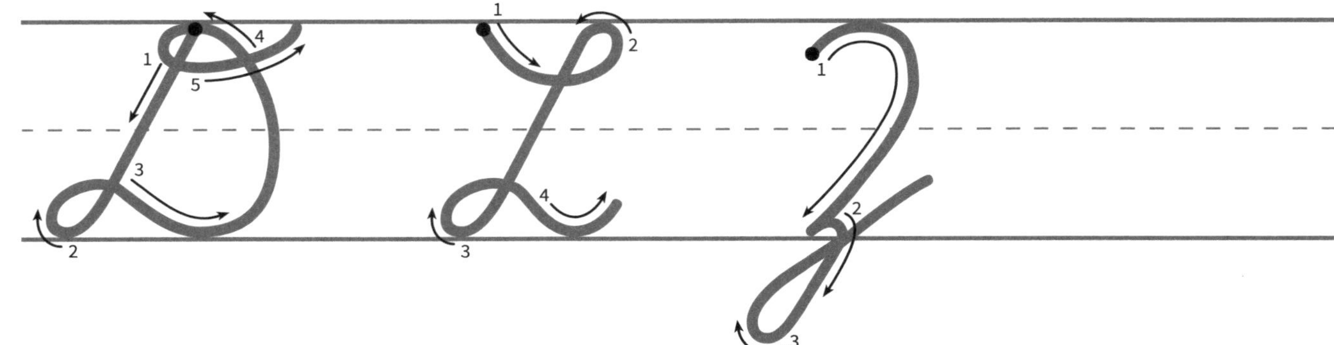

TRACE

WRITE

TRACE **WRITE**

TRACE **WRITE**

OVER, BACK-TRACE LOOP LEFT, DOWNSTROKE SWING RIGHT MOUND ROUND

acdgqofhklebijjprstuuwmnnxyzv

TRACE

Answer to a Child's Question

by Samuel Taylor Coleridge

Do you ask what the birds say?

The sparrow, the dove,

The linnet and thrush say,

"I love and I love!"

In the winter they're silent –
the wind is so strong;
What it says, I don't know,
but it sings a loud song.

Answer to a Child's Question
by Samuel Taylor Coleridge
Do you ask what the birds say?
The sparrow, the dove,
The linnet and thrush say,
"I love and I love!"

WRITE

OVER, BACK-TRACE LOOP LEFT, DOWNSTROKE SWING RIGHT MOUND ROUND

acdgqofhklebijprstuwvmnxyzv

TRACE

Leap Year Poem by Mother Goose

Thirty days hath September,
April, June and November.
All the rest have thirty-one,
Excepting February alone,
And that has twenty-eight days clear
And twenty-nine in each leap year.

Leap Year Poem by Mother Goose
Thirty days hath September,
April, June and November.
All the rest have thirty-one,
Excepting February alone,
And that has twenty-eight days clear
And twenty-nine in each leap year.

WRITE

acdgqofhklebijprstuwmnxyzv

TRACE

Clouds by Christina Rossetti

White sheep, white sheep,

On a blue hill,

When the wind stops,

You all stand still.

When the wind blows,

You walk away slow.

White sheep, white sheep,

Where do you go?

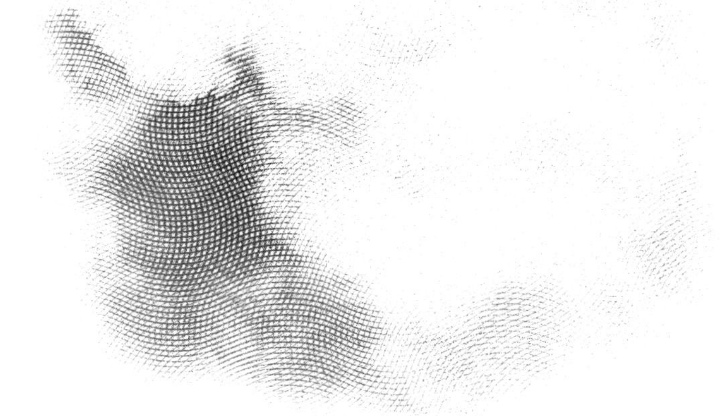

CHECK YOURSELF: ☐ Posture, Paper ☐ Triangle Hold ☐ Relaxed Hand, Light Pressure ☐ Touching the Guidelines Precisely ☐ Slant and Connections

WRITE

Clouds by Christina Rossetti

White sheep, white sheep,

On a blue hill,

When the wind stops,

You all stand still.

When the wind blows,

You walk away slow.

White sheep, white sheep,

Where do you go?

OVER, BACK-TRACE | LOOP LEFT, DOWNSTROKE | SWING RIGHT | MOUND ROUND

acdgqofhklebijprstuwmnxyzv

TRACE

Flint by Christina Rossetti

An emerald is as green as grass;

A ruby red as blood;

A sapphire shines as blue as heaven;

A flint lies in the mud.

CHECK YOURSELF: ☐ Posture, Paper ☐ Triangle Hold  ☐ Relaxed Hand, Light Pressure  ☐ Touching the Guidelines Precisely  ☐ Slant and Connections

A diamond is a brillant stone,
To catch the world's desire;
An opal holds a fiery spark;
But a flint holds fire.

WRITE

OVER, BACK-TRACE LOOP LEFT, DOWNSTROKE SWING RIGHT MOUND ROUND

acdggofhklebijjprstuwmnxyzv

TRACE

Little Things by Julia A. Carney

Little drops of water,

Little grains of sand,

Make the mighty ocean,

And the pleasant land.

And little deeds of kindness,

Little words of love,

Make our little earth below,

Like the heaven above.

CHECK YOURSELF: ☐ Posture, Paper ☐ Triangle Hold ☐ Relaxed Hand, Light Pressure ☐ Touching the Guidelines Precisely ☐ Slant and Connections

Little Things by Julia A. Carney

WRITE

WRITE

Little drops of water,
Little grains of sand,
Make the mighty ocean,
And the pleasant land.

And little deeds of kindness,
Little words of love,
Make our little earth below,
Like the heaven above.

acdgqofhklebijprstuwvmnxyzv

TRACE

The Rainbow

by Christina Rossetti

Boats sail on the rivers,

And ships sail on the seas;

But clouds that sail across the sky

Are prettier far than these.

CHECK YOURSELF: ☐ Posture, Paper ☐ Triangle Hold ☐ Relaxed Hand, Light Pressure ☐ Touching the Guidelines Precisely ☐ Slant and Connections

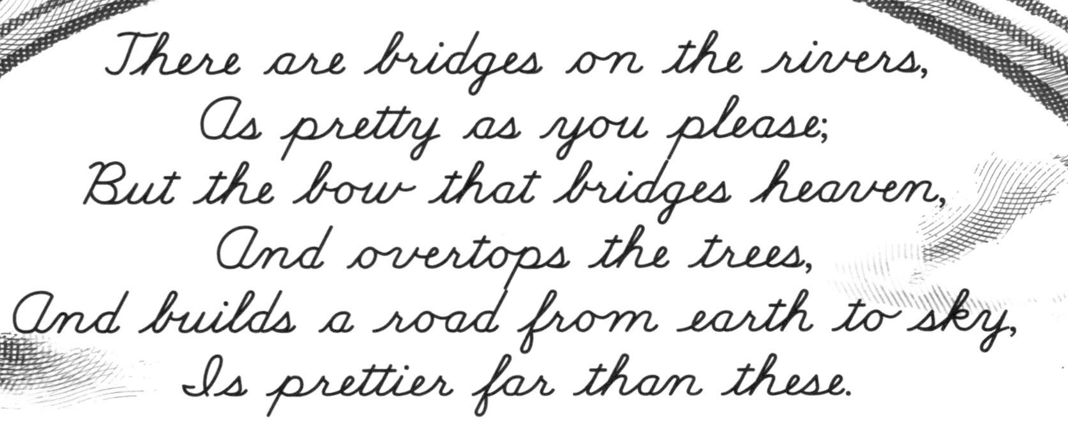

There are bridges on the rivers,
As pretty as you please;
But the bow that bridges heaven,
And overtops the trees,
And builds a road from earth to sky,
Is prettier far than these.

WRITE

OVER, BACK-TRACE LOOP LEFT, DOWNSTROKE SWING RIGHT MOUND ROUND

acdggofhkleb ijprstuwmnxyzv

TRACE

The Wind by Christina Rossetti

Who has seen the wind?

Neither I nor you:

But when the leaves hang trembling

The wind is passing through.

Who has seen the wind?

Neither you nor I:

But when the trees bow down their heads

The wind is passing by.

CHECK YOURSELF: ☐ Posture, Paper ☐ Triangle Hold ☐ Relaxed Hand, Light Pressure ☐ Touching the Guidelines Precisely ☐ Slant and Connections

The Wind by Christina Rossetti
Who has seen the wind?
Neither I nor you:
But when the leaves hang trembling
The wind is passing through.

WRITE

acdggofhklebijjprstuiwmnxyzv

TRACE

Caterpillar by Christina Rossetti

Brown and furry

Caterpillar in a hurry,

Take your walk

To the shady leaf, or stalk,

Or what not,

Which may be the chosen spot.

No toad spy you,
Hovering bird of prey pass by you;
Spin and die,
To live again a butterfly.

CHECK YOURSELF: Posture, Paper | Triangle Hold | Relaxed Hand, Light Pressure | Touching the Guidelines Precisely | Slant and Connections

Caterpillar by Christina Rossetti
Brown and furry
Caterpillar in a hurry,
Take your walk
To the shady leaf, or stalk,
Or what not,
Which may be the chosen spot.

WRITE

OVER, BACK-TRACE LOOP LEFT, DOWNSTROKE SWING RIGHT MOUND ROUND

acdgqofhklebijprstuwmnxyzv

TRACE

The Crocodile by Lewis Carroll

How doth the little crocodile

Improve his shining tail,

And pour the waters of the Nile

On every golden scale!

How cheerfully he seems to grin,

How neatly spreads his claws,

And welcomes little fishes in,

With gently smiling jaws!

CHECK YOURSELF: ☐ Posture, Paper ☐ Triangle Hold ☐ Relaxed Hand, Light Pressure ☐ Touching the Guidelines Precisely ☐ Slant and Connections

The Crocodile Lewis Carroll

How doth the little crocodile
Improve his shining tail,
And pour the waters of the Nile
On every golden scale!

How cheerfully he seems to grin,
How neatly spreads his claws,
And welcomes little fishes in,
With gently smiling jaws!

WRITE

acdggofhklebijjprstuiwmnxyzv

TRACE

Eletelephony by Laura Elizabeth Richards

Once there was an elephant,

Who tried to use the telephant—

No! No! I mean an elephone

Who tried to use the telephone—

(Dear me! I am not certain quite
That even now I've got it right.)
Howe'er it was, he got his trunk
Entangled in the telephunk;

The more he tried to get it free,
The louder buzzed the telephee—
(I fear I'd better drop the song
Of elephop and telephong!)

Eletelephony by Laura Elizabeth Richards

Once there was an elephant,
Who tried to use the telephant –
No! No! I mean an elephone
Who tried to use the telephone –

WRITE

OVER, BACK-TRACE LOOP LEFT, DOWNSTROKE SWING RIGHT MOUND ROUND

acdgqofhklebijprstuwvmnxyzv

TRACE

The Purple Cow by Gelett Burgess

I never saw a Purple Cow,

I never hope to see one,

But I can tell you, anyhow,

I'd rather see than be one!

The Purple Cow by Gelett Burgess

I never saw a Purple Cow,
I never hope to see one,
But I can tell you, anyhow,
I'd rather see than be one!

WRITE

OVER, BACK-TRACE | LOOP LEFT, DOWNSTROKE | SWING RIGHT | MOUND ROUND

acdgqofhklebijprstuwmnxyzv

TRACE

Star Spangled Banner

Francis Scott Key

O say can you see,

by the dawn's early light,

What so proudly we hail'd

at the twilight's last gleaming,

Whose broad stripes and bright stars
through the perilous fight
O'er the ramparts we watch'd
were so gallantly streaming?

CHECK YOURSELF: ☐ Posture, Paper ☐ Triangle Hold ☐ Relaxed Hand, Light Pressure ☐ Touching the Guidelines Precisely ☐ Slant and Connections

And the rocket's red glare,
the bombs bursting in air
Gave proof through the night
that our flag was still there,

WRITE

O say does that star-spangled
banner yet wave
O'er the land of the free
and the home of the brave?

OVER, BACK-TRACE LOOP LEFT, DOWNSTROKE SWING RIGHT MOUND ROUND

acdggofhkklebijjprstuwmnxyyzv

TRACE

This Land is Your Land

Woody Guthrie

This land is your land,

This land is my land,

From California

To the New York Island,

From the redwood forest,

To the Gulf Stream waters,

This land was made for you and me.

CHECK YOURSELF: ☐ Posture, Paper ☐ Triangle Hold ☐ Relaxed Hand, Light Pressure ☐ Touching the Guidelines Precisely ☐ Slant and Connections

As I was walking,
That ribbon of highway,
I saw above me
That endless skyway,
I saw below me
That golden valley.
This land was made for you and me.

WRITE

OVER, BACK-TRACE LOOP LEFT, DOWNSTROKE **SWING RIGHT** MOUND ROUND

acdgqofhkleb ijprstuw vmnxyz v

TRACE

You're a Grand Old Flag

George M. Cohan

You're a grand old flag,

You're a high-flying flag,

And forever in peace may you wave.

You're the emblem of the land I love,

The home of the free and the brave.

Ev'ry heart beats true
'Neath the Red, White and Blue,
Where there's never a boast or brag.
But should auld acquaintance be forgot,
Keep your eye on the grand old flag.

WRITE